BUT I'M NOT AN EXPERT!

BUT I'M NOT AN EXPERT!

Go from newbie to expert and radically skyrocket your online influence without feeling like a fraud

MEERA KOTHAND

BUT I'M NOT AN EXPERT!

Go from newbie to expert and radically skyrocket your influence without feeling like a fraud

MEERA KOTHAND
WWW.MEERAKOTHAND.COM

COPYRIGHT © 2018

CONTENTS PAGE

You can download the Instant Expert pack at https://nowanexpert.com/bonus.

INTRODUCTION

THE BIG, BOLD PROMISE

But I'm not an expert...

These are the words written and spoken by hundreds of readers I've had the opportunity of interacting with over the years.

Maybe you've uttered these words yourself.

Or entertained them in your head.

You're new...

You want to start a business online...

You want to create content to attract an audience...

You want to speak, write, create, and sell, but the only thing stopping you in your tracks is fear.

Fear, that you're not an expert.

You don't have the years of experience to prove your worth.

Or testimonials in the hundreds that you can pick from.

Why would anyone listen to you when you're not an expert?

Why would anyone pay attention when you might as well be this tiny speck among the thousands of online businesses out there?

Well, we're going to change that.

The aim of this book is not to make you the best in your expert niche, but to help you recognize where you stand and how you can boost your expertise in the eyes of the people you want to serve—the people whom your business is for.

But if you think that I'll be revealing the secret that's usually found behind a $3,000 paywall...

Or the genius hack that only six- and seven-figure entrepreneurs know of...

Or the one-of-a-kind marketing *trick* that's going to make people *believe* you're an expert...

Then you may be disappointed.

Yes, you'll know exactly what you need to do in a 180-day push to start branding yourself as an expert.

Yes, you'll build a marketing campaign that you can take and run with at the end.

You'll also know how to apply minimum viable formulas—the bare-bones framework you need to get started in email marketing, creating content, and more, especially if you're time starved and don't have eight hours a day to build an expert business or side hustle.

But the strategies and hacks here are not gimmicks or secrets.

You don't ever have to *fake* being an expert either.

These are intentional, calculated steps that you can take, and this book will give you a plan for how you can get there.

First, let's get the definitions out of the way.

Who is an expert?

An expert is someone who has acquired knowledge and skills through study and practice over the years, in a particular field or subject, to the extent that his or her opinion may be helpful in fact finding, problem solving, or understanding of a situation.[1]

Some say an expert is someone who has spent at least 10,000 hours studying or learning about a particular topic. But the definition of what and who an expert is, is relative.

There isn't a fixed, absolute definition for what it takes to become one. Sure, in some professional fields there are recognized qualifications. But in several online business niches there are none, and we still recognize and identify some people as trusted experts.

Who is an influencer or micro-influencer?

According to an article by InfluencerBay,[2] influencers have followers of 1 million+ whereas micro-influencers have 1,000+ followers. The key thing to note is that micro-influencers have more trust, higher engagement, and greater impact.

The article aligns with a study by Collective Bias.[3] Their research of over 14,000 online users showed that only 3% of people would consider buying a product if it was endorsed by a celebrity. But 30% of people are more likely to purchase a product based on a recommendation from a non-celebrity blogger than a celebrity.

So, while both segments can influence purchasing decisions, micro-influencers (YOU!) have the ability to build trust with their audience. So even if you have a small audience or are starting from scratch, you're not a fraud for wanting to position yourself as an expert.

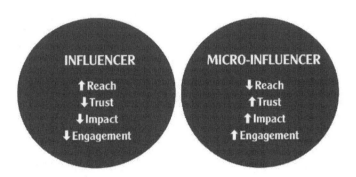

This sweet spot—where you've established rapport with your audience, have a high engagement rate, are able to impact purchasing decisions, and have built trust because you don't just "know your stuff" but are seen as someone who truly understands their problems—is where you want to be.

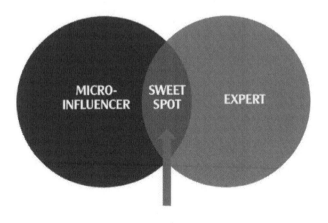

First, let's unpack what makes an expert.

UNCOVERING THE EXPERT QUOTIENT

Expert Quotient = Knowledge + Authority Architecture + Marketability

The diagram below shows the three different components you need to consider before you start branding yourself as an expert. In this book, you'll discover what it takes to build up each of these components.

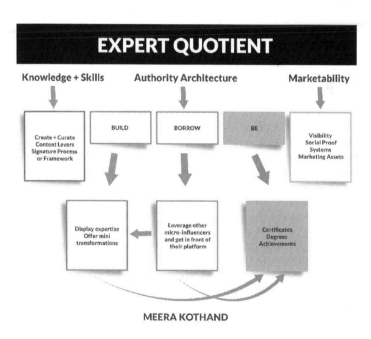

MEERA KOTHAND

The **Knowledge** component is all about how you create and curate content to demonstrate your expertise and attract and retain your ideal customers. In this section, you'll discover how to quickly pick up knowledge in your expert niche even if you're starting from scratch.

The second component, **Authority Architecture**, shows you three different pathways to garnering authority—build, borrow, and be. Several people have written about steps and methods to establish authority in your field, including author Steve Scott who mentions the 3 B's of Authority in his book *How to Find a Profitable Blog Topic Idea*.[4] Most of the strategies and methods surrounding authority can be categorized into these three different pathways.

To **"be" the authority** is the hardest aspect because you've got to have the credentials, achievements, professional qualifications, or years of experience to show for it. Perhaps you've built businesses in your expert niche for ten years or worked for Fortune 100 companies. The majority of people don't start here, which is why I have that portion of the diagram grayed out.

Let's focus on the "build" and "borrow" aspects of the authority architecture. You **build authority** when you demonstrate your expertise through events such as challenges or live coaching. You also build authority when you share your progress online. If you're on a mission to help people lose weight, you document your progress even though you haven't "made it" yet. Notice an explosion in personal brands tracking their quarterly or monthly progress through income reports, Instagram stories, or behind-the-scenes pictures? Those are examples of building authority.

Borrowing authority is when you leverage other micro-influencers' and influencers' platforms to get in front of their audience. You siphon some of their credibility by associating with the clout their brand has built up.

But these don't work in silos.

As you build and borrow authority, you start *being* the authority. Your audience starts to view you as one. The arrows in the diagram symbolize the flows between these three different methods, which we'll cover in the book.

But how you present and **market** yourself pulls the authority and knowledge elements together to reinforce and cement your position as an expert in the minds of your readers and ideal customers. So all three pillars in the expert quotient are important as you set out to position yourself as an expert.

Some of you may be skeptical...

Is being seen as an expert really that important?

It depends on the type of business you want to build. Are you building an expert business—a business built by sharing your expertise with others? Will your business benefit by you having the expert tag?

If you have doubts about the need to position yourself as an expert, here are some of the benefits of building an expert business.

WHY IS BEING AN EXPERT IMPORTANT?

1. You can enjoy word-of-mouth marketing

Once you're an expert in a particular niche, you get "tagged" in social conversations. People refer others to you because you specialize in a particular area or do work that's tailored for a particular audience. You make it easy for them to say "Emma's great at this. She's worked with plenty of designers just like you. Reach out to her."

There has to be a degree of KNOW-LIKE-TRUST for someone to recommend you or refer you to others. But that degree of trust can be built up through content as you'll see later on in the book.

2. You can attract your ideal prospects, and it's easier to convert them to customers

You'll be able to get laser focused with your website and other marketing materials because you're clear about who exactly you're attracting and how you're helping them. This strengthens your marketability and branding and, in turn, creates a snowball effect and attracts more ideal customers to you.

Have a look at the table below.

If you're self-publishing your first book and everything about the process scares you, who are you more likely to call for help? The generalist virtual assistant (VA) or the VA who specializes in book publishing-related tasks. Similarly, if you have an upcoming product launch and have a whole bunch of tech systems you need to set up and sync with your payment gateway and course dashboard, which of these people will you most likely hire?

VA	Constantly busy with everyday business tasks? I can help you with anything you need to free up time for that passion project.
Tech VA	Have a bunch of techy tasks that you want forgotten? I'm a tech VA and specialize in techy tasks. Here is a list of tools I have experience using: Slack, Zapier, Leadpages, and Drip. Tech and systems are my passion, but they don't have to be yours. Let me take them off your plate.
VA for Authors	I specialize in freeing up time for authors like you so that you can do what you do best—write. Let me handle everything else that takes you away from your writing. Here are some of the

	things I can help you with: research, beta reading, book promotion, securing ISBN numbers, etc.

3. You can differentiate yourself from competitors

Have a look at any business coach or service provider's site and you'll likely see the following themes running through their "work with me" or sales page.

- Actionable content
- Results driven process
- Prompt customer service
- Videos, downloads, swipe files, workbooks

But these are points of parity. Points of parity are elements that are mandatory—that everyone operating in that space should have—for them to *even* be considered by potential customers. These don't make your business different.

Your points of differentiation do.

Points of differentiation are the attributes that make your brand unique. They are what make up your competitive advantage.

4. You can easily form joint ventures, collaborations, and partnerships

When I was looking for guest experts to complement the content in one of my paid products, I sought help from other experts in Pinterest management, video marketing, and automation. Likewise, Jen A. Miller, the founder of Toast Meets Jam and a brand strategist, reached out to me a couple of months ago because she realized that most of her branding students wanted to learn more about email marketing. While she has experience running her own email campaigns, she wanted to bring me in because that is my area of specialization.

By niching down, you open yourself up to collaborations and partnerships especially from other businesses who offer complementary services and products. Audiences on both sides will feel well taken care of because they are in the hands of experts.

5. You can charge a premium

You become highly sought after when you've been tagged as an expert for a skill set that an audience is seeking, allowing you to command premium prices. People would rather work with an expert who has a deep understanding of their problem than someone who seems to solve everything under the sun. That's the difference between someone who charges $100 an hour and someone who charges $30 an hour.

But all of these reasons don't matter if you can't answer this next question.

Why is being an expert important to you?

Maybe you want to get invited to speak at conferences and events...

Or you love the rush of being featured on high-profile sites...

Or you want to get paid for your expertise and be able to charge a premium...

Maybe your business model (your primary method of earning an income) will benefit from you having an expert tag...

All of these are great reasons to want to be seen as an expert. But you have to do it because *you* have a plausible reason and want to, *not* because everyone says you have to do so. You need to know what becoming an expert means to *you*. Because why I want to be seen as an expert and what it means to me will differ from what it means to you.

To me, it could mean being able to get more speaking opportunities. To you, it could be the ability to work with selective clients on your own terms.

Whatever your reason is, hold on to your why.

It will help you in the last section as you plot out your marketing plan.

Maybe you think you are hopeless right now...

Your niche doesn't see you as an expert...

Your audience or subscribers don't see you as an expert either...

Maybe you're brand new and haven't even zeroed in on what you want "your thing" to be...

Take a deep breath, because it's ok!

This book assumes that you're starting afresh.

Rules for how you should read this book?

Just one. Trust in the process. I crash tested every single one of these strategies myself when I was completely new to the online space.

And it *is* possible to start on a clean slate, stake a claim to a niche, and be seen as the go-to expert with time.

Whatever your reason is for picking up a copy of this book, you *will* walk away with ideas to market and "sell" yourself as an expert. You may even be surprised at how quickly your audience starts to view you as one by implementing these strategies and techniques.

If you're intrigued and ready, let's go!

SECTION I

PICKING YOUR EXPERT NICHE

You're now convinced that it's possible to position yourself as an expert.

But what if you haven't the faintest clue as to what your expert niche should be...

Or what if you're undecided about the niche that's right for you?

In this section, you'll decide how to pick and validate the right expert niche. You'll also read case studies from different solopreneurs about how they nailed their expert niche.

CHAPTER 1

IDENTIFYING "YOUR THING"

What is an expert niche?

And is it the same as your target market?

Target market and niche are often used interchangeably, but they're not the same thing. A target market is the specific group of people you want to serve. A niche, on the other hand, is the expertise you specialize in offering this target market.

Choosing your expert niche is a three-fold decision that involves YOU, the marketplace, and your audience.

An ideal expert niche is one where there's a match between a hungry market that is actively looking for help with solving a specific set of problems and your ability to deliver what they want.

But is it right for your expert niche to be in something like marketing or fitness or food? Let take's the example of marketing. There are so many different types of marketing—such as email marketing, SEO, video marketing, mobile marketing, and Facebook ads. Can someone really be an expert in all of this?

Not quite. Not unless you're someone like Neil Patel who has over ten years' experience under his belt and more than 4,000 blog posts where he has perfected his craft.[5]

Here are some critical factors to consider when choosing the right expert niche.

YOUR AUDIENCE

1. Are people actively looking for solutions to the problems associated with your niche? And are they willing to pay for it? Are there **money flows** within your niche?

Most solopreneurs think of digital products when they consider money flows. But these money flows can be in consulting, coaching, services, affiliate marketing, masterminds, live events and workshops, conferences, and even physical products.

If you're unable to wrap your head around the idea of solving problems, consider if your niche helps people become better versions of themselves or gives them something that they want but don't have. This better version also doesn't have to be about making more money. It could be in areas such as personal development, food, personal finance, and fashion/beauty, as well as lifestyle which includes travel, outdoor/survival, and home decor. Each of these topics can also encompass a wide range of subniches.

2. Is this an urgent problem that they need solved?

In the book *80/20 Sales and Marketing*,[6] Perry Marshall calls this the bleeding neck. This is a "dire sense of urgency, an immediate problem that demands to be solved. Right. Now." The more urgent and pressing the problem, the more in demand your business will be.

Case Study 1

Joan has worked for several companies on their digital marketing strategy. She wanted to start her own online business, but she didn't want to be another digital marketing strategist. She also couldn't feature testimonials or reviews from the companies she has worked for due to confidentiality agreements. She was pretty much starting afresh.

Her specialty was content marketing, but there were several businesses and experts offering content marketing services. She decided to drill down into one aspect of content marketing that she delivered the best—storytelling. She realized that there is a huge demand for it and that most online businesses don't know how to do this well or even how to start. She branded her business with the tagline "helping tiny online businesses tell better stories" and started offering high-touch consulting services.

MARKETPLACE

1. Are there others who have successfully monetized this niche regardless of the business model they used?

2. Is there a big enough marketplace for it? Heard of the saying: money follows passion? That's not always true especially if there isn't a large enough marketplace of paying clients or customers to sustain that passion.

Two tools that are my go-to for market research are AnswerThePublic[7] and Ubersuggest[8]. In Ubersuggest, you can enter keywords related to your expert niche and it shows you search volumes as well as related search phrases.

In AnswerThePublic, the tool takes the keywords you enter and presents related questions that people search on Google. It maps out the questions into a diagram like that below.

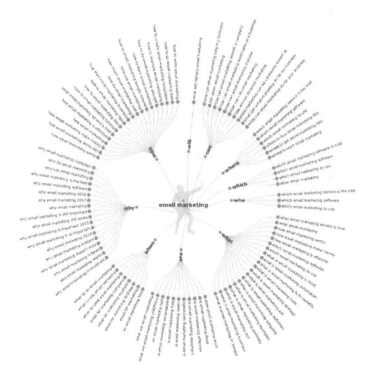

YOU

1. Can you see yourself writing about or researching this expert niche for the next 3–5 years? Are you eager to learn more about it?

2. Do you want to be associated with this expert niche for the next 3–5 years?

3. What type of clients or audience do you love working with?

4. Are you able to reach your audience? What social platforms will you use to find them? What social media platforms do they use? What websites do they read? If you can't connect with them or reach them, they'll never be able to do business with you.

If you've considered these questions, you're bound to have identified a few niches.

This is where you narrow it down to **one.** The following questions will help:

- What are you already known for?

- What are you most excited about specializing in?

- Where can you establish yourself with the least amount of effort?

- Is this a niche that has a growing demand?

- Is this a niche that is poorly served by competitors or existing players in the market? Is there an **opportunity gap** that you can fill?

  Consider the audience you are serving and the content available to them before you answer this question. For instance, there is plenty of email marketing advice for B2B firms and huge companies but hardly any in-depth information tailored to personal brands and solopreneurs. That was an opportunity gap that I wanted to fill.

If you've carefully considered these questions, you should have now identified your expert niche.

But this is where most of the subscribers or clients I speak to are scared.

They're scared of turning people away because they offer something that's too specialized.

They're scared of becoming unattractive to clients who want help with a broader set of services.

Sure, choosing an expert niche means turning some people away, but you also become the obvious choice for people looking to solve a specific problem. You stop competing on price and it becomes incredibly easier to focus your marketing and have it speak clearly to a hungry market.

Case Study 2

Sarah always had an interest in exploring different types of food and finding out their origins. She also considered herself a history buff. She was especially fascinated with her grandmother's recipes and where they were passed down from. She naturally wanted to create a business around her passion. She wanted to start creating content and then transition into cookbooks and videos. But she didn't want to create another food blog. There were thousands of them around.

She started looking at what people were asking about and what she had an interest in as well. She

---

came across the ketogenic food niche and decided to zone in on that. But she didn't just share recipes and videos, she also infused her love of history and talked about how her recipes were inspired by different types of cultures and where they originated from. Having such a targeted niche and specific type of reader, she is able to attract sponsorships from companies who want to work with online entrepreneurs with a keto-centric audience like hers. She also has a book in the works.

Action Item:

1. Determine what you want to become the go-to expert for. To help you with this, there is a set of worksheets you can download at https://nowanexpert.com/bonus.

SECTION II

STAKING CLAIM TO YOUR EXPERT
STATUS WITH KNOWLEDGE

Knowledge breeds confidence, right?

The best way for you to be recognized as an expert is by creating amazing content. The more knowledge you are seen to have about the topic, the quicker you build credibility. You'll also have more confidence to talk and share about the topic on any platform.

When your content directly shows how much you truly understand the problems of your target market, your audience will also naturally look to you as their solution.

But how much knowledge do you truly need to present yourself as an expert in the niche? What type of content do you need to create so that you're able to do so? In this section, you'll look at two aspects of content that help to position you as an expert: content creation and content curation. You'll also discover the most neglected content type and how it affects your efforts in building an expert business.

CHAPTER 2

CREATE VALUABLE CONTENT THAT POSITIONS YOU AS AN EXPERT

What exactly is value?

Most people associate massive free guides, downloads, lengthy how-to content, and tutorials as value.

But value is more than that.

Value is changing perceptions and mindsets.

Value is being the person your audience turns to, to make sense of it all.

The person who shows them not just what they could do, but what they *should* do.

Is this more difficult than sending your audience a link to a post or email on "10 Must-Have Hacks to Do Something"?

You bet it is!

Valuable content also *adds* to the body of literature or content already present in this niche.

This is where most people panic because they associate this with coming up with original ideas. They throw up their hands and say it's impossible.

I agree.

Nothing is original anymore and pretty much everything has been done. If you think of a topic, it's highly likely someone (think a hundred people or more) has already written about it.

The idea is not to be radically original. The idea is to differentiate yourself.

Many of the existing content pieces in your niche may be detailed or long-form content. Does this mean you need to go longer or better than existing pieces of content?

No, you don't.

You'll also never be able to out-do those larger sites or agencies who publish daily articles and extensive guides because they have an entire team of writers. You shouldn't be competing with them in the first place. Your content doesn't have to be long to add to the conversation. So don't think of *add* in terms of word count. Think of *add* in terms of a new angle, perspective, or strategy that will be considered valuable.

CONTENT LEVERS

There are three characteristics of content that are deemed valuable. I like to think of these as content levers.

1. Breaks sacred cows

Sacred cow is an idiom that refers to something immune to criticism or questions. What do you silently loathe or disagree with in your niche? What beliefs are your target audience holding on to that are limiting them? Pick out myths and beliefs that are immune to criticism or questions. Prove these wrong. Let your hunches, your nudges, your "huh" moments lead you.

Infuse these into your content. These are what myth and mistake posts are made up of.

2. Has a clearly identifiable point of view

Valuable content is content that takes a stance about the topics and problems in your niche. These views could be polarizing to a certain extent, but that's what makes people decide whether to follow you and continue to read your content. These are what opinion posts are made up of.

Note: You can break sacred cows and have a clearly identifiable point of view, but if you don't have the credibility or authority to show for it yet, it can quickly come across as a rant. That doesn't mean you have to shy away from writing opinionated posts. It just means that you need to show examples and substantiate your content with third-party sources such as reputable articles and quotes from authoritative sources.

3. Fills an opportunity gap

Valuable content addresses frequently asked questions that the competition hasn't adequately addressed. It also provides another viewpoint or angle in answering these questions.

CONTENT PIECES TO CLAIM EXPERT STATUS

The below examples are the types of content pieces that work really well to claim expert status. If you notice, they align with the above characteristics as well. I have also given you examples of the content pieces I've written that correspond with each type.

	Pros	Cons
1. Polarizing posts or opinion posts—e.g., What they're not telling you about... Everything that's wrong about... E.g., 13 myths you believe about launching your blog & online business (but	A chance to wow your audience if you write it well. Gives light bulb moments and immediately grabs their attention.	If you don't substantiate it with evidence or don't clarify your points, it may come across as a rant rather than a well thought out conversation. If you don't have social proof or authority, this

never ever should)		post may fall flat at first and may take time to build sufficient traffic.
2. Questions that your ideal customer is asking, but the competition has failed to address or *adequately* address E.g., What to send your email list: The beginner's guide for the clueless blogger	You gain their trust and get reactions such as *This is exactly what I was looking for. Wish I had found your post sooner.*	-
3. How-to content E.g., How to grow your tiny email list with 29	This is the staple of most blogs. There are always newbies looking for how-to	There are likely to already be similar content pieces. You have to position your

simple but powerful tactics	content to address their common questions.	post in a different angle to get attention, starting with your headline.
4. Common topic but with an opportunity gap E.g., Does your opt-in freebie suck? Here's how to create one that converts like crazy	You gain their trust because you're sharing a viewpoint or angle that they have most likely never read before.	There are likely posts that already exist on this topic. For your post to not be seen as noise, you need to get your audience's attention quickly by calling out the solution that the other content pieces give and why those don't actually help them in any way.

CREATE MIDDLE OF FUNNEL CONTENT

At any time, there are one of six people interacting with your brand: Stranger – Reader – Subscriber – Engaged Subscriber – Customer & Brand Advocate. A marketing funnel is the pathway by which someone goes from Stranger to Brand Advocate.

The top of the funnel reflects people who are becoming aware of your brand and the bottom reflects your paying customers. The funnel becomes narrower further down because not everyone will become a paying customer. The aim of your content should be to move people further down the funnel.

Top of Funnel	
Stranger	They haven't heard of you before at all. They probably clicked to your site from seeing a pin image on Pinterest, a Facebook post that a friend of theirs shared, or a tweet on their Twitter feed.
Reader	They have some form of brand recognition. They've heard of you before via a podcast or seen your guest post on a site they frequent. A friend of theirs has been raving about you. They've clicked through to your site to read your content.
Subscriber	They are new to your list. They visit your site likely from a link in your welcome email series. They may have read something intriguing in your sequence of emails and wanted to have a look at your blog, YouTube channel, or other content platforms.

Engaged subscriber	Heard of a brand crush? That's what these people have on you. They adore your style. Most of them cannot wait to get their hands on your paid products if they haven't already.
Customer & Brand advocate	These are people who are attuned to your style. They've likely bought from you before—possibly more than once.
Bottom of Funnel	

The diagram below shows the various types of content that will attract your ideal reader or customer at different stages.

ATTRACT (AWARENESS)
Guest Posts, Podcasts, Social Media, Paid Traffic, Referrals, Summits, Events and Workshops

CAPTURE (INTEREST)
Lead Magnets, Content Upgrades, Blog Posts, Landing Pages

ENGAGE (CONSIDERATION)
Challenges, Email Sequences, Webinars, Workshops, Newsletters & Emails, Nurture Sequences

CONVERT (PURCHASE)
Sales Sequence, Client Calls

RETAIN (REPEAT PURCHASE)
Affiliate Program, Sneak Peaks, Special Deals

While every stage of the funnel is important, the middle is the one that's most often neglected. Most solopreneurs I work with tend to pay attention to bottom of funnel content, neglecting the middle. Or it only strikes them that they need to beef up the middle, four weeks before a massive launch.

But when you're trying to position yourself as an expert, the content you create in the middle can add the most value. When done well, the content here puts you ahead of the competition in the minds of your audience. You become the go-to person for everything related to the topic.

Why?

Because this is where people already identify with your brand. They are aware of you but are still discovering more about the problem and how you possibly fit in as a solution. This is also where your content can spur dialogue and conversation without being salesy. You get to earn the attention of people and position yourself as a solution to their problems.

Email is a key medium that delivers most of the middle of funnel content. A McKinsey & Company study found that email is **forty times** more effective than Facebook and Twitter combined.[9] An email subscriber is more valuable than a social media follower. Because if you had 1,000 followers, 1,000 organic visitors, and 1,000 email subscribers, and you tried to sell to all of them, you could expect to convert 6 followers, 25 visitors, and 42 subscribers.[10] Email also gives the highest return on investment (ROI) of $44 for every dollar spent. So it has to be a part of your content strategy.

If you're overwhelmed wondering how you're going to start creating middle of funnel content or how to start incorporating the recommended expert content pieces, don't be! This is where you can implement what I call the minimum viable formulas for email marketing, your blog, and your content. We'll discuss this in the next chapter.

Need help with email marketing?
Sign up for my free course at
https://meera.email/course.

LEARN CONTINUOUSLY

The key to feeling like an expert is to have enough knowledge to feel confident discussing the topic. You don't have to be the world's leading expert on the topic, but you do need to build up your own pool of knowledge and commit to continuously learning about it. You also need to understand your own level of experience and the level of the people you are marketing to.

If you're marketing to beginners, you want to be two steps ahead of them and dig into intermediate and advanced content. You want to read books, podcasts, and industry blogs that they are unlikely to read.

But how do you do this amid all the other tasks involved in setting up a business? The usual complaint is that there isn't enough time to read so much material. Here are some quick hacks to streamline how you acquire knowledge as well as find resources.

Identify existing resources in your niche

Who are the existing experts in your niche?

Create a list of 5–10 experts.

Now identify their work.

Have they written any books? Check on Amazon. If they haven't published a book, find out which books they consider essential or what's on their reading lists. Have a look at the expert's website or blog, search for any videos on YouTube, look for their podcasts on iTunes, and join their email lists.

Here's a method that I use to read 1–2 nonfiction books a week. You don't have to read a book cover to cover to get the most out of it. I highly recommend that you don't. Most people who read several books a week or month employ variations of the method I use below:

- Read the synopsis or blurb of the book. Look at the back cover or the book description.
- Take a helicopter view by scanning the table of contents.
  - Identify the chapters that appear most useful to you.
  - What chapters or section headings seem interesting?
    - Create an overview using a three-layer process.

o   Write out the headings within the chapters.

o   Then flesh out the headings with subheads.

o   Go deeper by adding in phrases that are in bold, italics, or make reference to flowcharts or diagrams. These help you quickly grasp information.

I usually use a notebook and pen to make a mind map following the steps above, but you can also use free tools like MindMeister. Here's a snapshot of what this method of reading and analyzing the book *Essentialism: The Disciplined Pursuit of Less* by Greg McKeown would look like on a mind mapping tool.

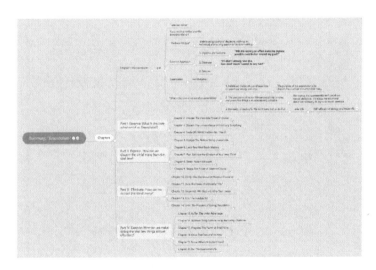

Source:
https://www.mindmeister.com/528724045/summa
ry-essentialism#

BuzzSumo[11] is another perfect avenue for identifying key resources.

Head over to BuzzSumo.com. Key in a search phrase related to your expert niche. Click on Content Analysis followed by Search. Scroll down to the most shared domains by network. You'll be able to see which websites, blogs, and publications are receiving the most shares. This requires a pro subscription to BuzzSumo though.

But you can still get data by doing a normal search on BuzzSumo. You will see the top content based on shares. Take down these sites and look for related posts on the same topics. Then quickly skim each post, pulling out subheadings and highlighted words.

CREATE A CONTENT HUB AND BE "EVERYWHERE"

You want to quickly build up a body of content that reflects your approach to this niche so that you start attracting and educating an audience who comes to understand you, your brand, and your process as well as the challenges that they are facing. You also want them to associate you with this topic.

If you've read my book *The One Hour Content Plan*, you'll know that I talk about having different content buckets or categories.

So what about content in those other buckets and categories?

Do you just ignore them?

Do you have to be tied down to only creating content around this topic?

No, you don't.

But what we're trying to do here is quickly build high-quality content around this niche on a few different mediums and platforms so that people start to view you as an expert.

This gives the impression that you're "everywhere."

Does this mean you'll need to create content on a few different mediums or platforms?

You'll actually end up stretching yourself really thin if you do so. Which form of content comes most naturally to you? Which are you able to express yourself the best in? For some, it's audio or video. For others, it could be written. Pick one that you can be consistent in first before exploring other mediums. You can create the impression of being everywhere by *borrowing* others' platforms. We'll discuss this in the next section on authority architecture.

Should you have a blog?

It depends. A blog is not a magic switch.

Just because you have a blog doesn't mean you automatically have an upper hand. Whether you have a blog or use video or audio as a primary content channel, that medium only works if the content you create on it feeds your goals. In this case, the goals are to (**a**) position yourself as an expert, (**b**) attract people who need assistance with solving the problems your products and services (or future products and services) help with, and (**c**) sell your products and services.

If your content isn't related to any of these goals, you will waste significant time and resources creating content that doesn't make an impact on your goals in any way and attracts people who may never go on to become customers.

How often should you create content?

It depends. There are people who blog every day but write short, pithy posts of 300–500 words. Bernadette Jiwa at The Story of Telling[12] is the best example of this. There are others who write longer form content once a week or every fortnight. Some create a video every single day or once a week. Your audience will get used to your style and self-select. If you've never blogged before, start by sticking to a fortnightly publishing schedule.

On what social media platform should you promote your content?

Where do most of your ideal audience get their content from? Where do they look for information? If you're completely clueless, a quick hack is to head to SimilarWeb. Are there competitors who have an overlapping audience with the one you're trying to attract? Key in their website URL to get some data on the type of social traffic they get. This will give you an insight into which social channels their audience use and by default, which channels yours use.

If you want to dive into content deeper, have a look at *The One Hour Content Plan* (https://1hcp.me) and CREATE Planner (https://createplanner.com).

Case Study 3

Brenda has always had a keen interest in herbs and natural healing as well as yoga and Pilates. After the birth of her children, she suffered from postpartum depression as well as incontinence.

She couldn't find the right answers from anyone to heal her core and pelvic floor naturally. She took her passion for natural healing and yoga/Pilates and combined it to focus on rehabilitative exercises and natural remedies for postpartum women. She found a ready audience of women just like her seeking help in this area. She started her business with consulting and then went on to create a group program to help this audience.

DEVELOP A SIGNATURE PROCESS OR FRAMEWORK

Is there a unifying approach to your work in your expert niche?

Imagine a coach or course creator who has a proven, one-of-a-kind system that takes someone from A–Z in a topic. Everything they teach is based on this framework or process. Their thoughts or opinions are not haphazardly thrown together. Nor are they drifting and changing their take on the topic every single week. Having a connected framework evokes confidence in you and shows your knowledge, your investment of time in your craft, as well as your commitment to getting results for your audience. Examples of a signature process are Kendrick Shope's Authentic Selling® or the 5-Step Activation Process I teach in my course Email Lists Simplified™.

How can you develop your own signature process or framework? Start by mapping out all the steps or the overall path someone must take to achieve the promised result. How can you group these steps into categories, themes, or concepts?

Is this something that you will know immediately? Of course not.

Your signature process or framework will develop over time as you work with and teach more people in your audience.

CHAPTER 2A

MINIMUM VIABLE MARKETING FORMULA (PART 1)

You may have previously come across the term Minimum Viable Product (MVP). An MVP is a product in its most bare-bones form but that is still viable to start selling. Can you utilize the same concept for your marketing?

Yes, why not?

Having a bare-bones framework beats having none at all, and these are the foundational pillars that give your business that quick start.

I once had a subscriber mention that she was working on having twenty blog posts written in the back end of her site before she went live and launched her business. The problem here is two-fold:

a. When you feel the pressure to create 15–20 posts before you even launch, it creates immense resistance on top of everything else you're dealing with. You don't want to add to the resistance of launching a new business with a task that's as insurmountable as this. If you've read the book *The War of Art* by Steven Pressfield,[13] you'll know exactly what I'm talking about when I say *resistance*.

b. You're losing a huge amount of time by waiting to hit 15–20 posts. Time that you could use to grow your email list and your audience. Time that you could use to build credibility and authority. So you'll get a huge boost by starting with the minimum viable formula first.

MINIMUM VIABLE MARKETING FORMULAS

In this book, you'll see minimum viable marketing formulas covered in two parts. In this first part, you will cover minimum viable formulas for starting a blog/website, creating a content plan, and email marketing. These minimum viable formulas are not drawn out of thin air but based largely on instilling KNOW-LIKE-TRUST in your audience so that they come to see you as an expert in your niche.

KNOW – They need to be aware that you exist.

LIKE – They need to connect with your style and be open to what you have to say. In many cases, without a basic LIKE or connect, it's difficult to build trust.

TRUST – They need to trust that you can help them solve their problems—that you're the go-to for that topic.

Minimum Viable Content Plan

These are the content pieces I recommend having in your Minimum Viable Content Plan (MVCP). The plan can be used for your blog or any other content medium you are using. These content pieces will also align with the three content levers we discussed above: breaks sacred cows; fills an opportunity gap; has an identifiable point of view.

- Two how-to or list posts on a pressing question the competition has failed to address.

- One polarizing or opinion post; e.g., X things you should never believe about...Why is this flawed...What they don't ever tell you about...

It's also good to note that your content plan will evolve over time. Initially, when you're trying to get established, you may find yourself focusing more on borrowing authority and writing content for other platforms. As you establish expertise and start growing your own audience, you may find yourself creating more content on your chosen content medium rather than on other platforms. This is a natural progression.

Despite all this, you want to keep in mind that you need a solid number of new readers or "leads" entering your funnels every single month. Most businesses get too comfortable and busy taking care of existing clients or customers that they forget that their business needs a continuous stream of fresh eyeballs so that they always have a pipeline of potential customers who are excited and waiting to do business with them.

Minimum Viable Email Marketing

Your Minimum Viable Email Marketing (MVEM) consists of the following:

- One opt-in incentive or lead magnet
- One landing page for your opt-in incentive or lead magnet
- Opt-in forms on three top posts
- Check your Google Analytics to find out what these are. Head to Behavior > Site Content > All Pages
- One thank you page where you will direct new subscribers to click confirm that they do indeed want to subscribe to get your opt-in incentive
- One top bar/exit intent pop-up/slide-in to capture traffic
- One welcome email that covers the 3Cs
  - Credibility
    Who are you? Why should they trust you or listen to you? What logos, features, special life incidents, beliefs, or viewpoints will build up your credibility?
  - Context
    Why is what you're talking about important now?

o   Continuity

How can you create an open loop that keeps them looking forward to your next email? The postscript or P.S. is the best place to tease your next email in your nurture series or nurture funnel.

• Three emails in your nurture funnel

One myth or mistake email

o   The easiest way to get someone to trust you is to break a widely held myth or share something that gives them an "aha" or light bulb moment.

o   What breaks your heart or makes you cringe in your industry/niche?

o   What do your ideal readers believe that they shouldn't?

o   What's the biggest excuse they make?

o   Identify the sacred cows and then break them.

One quick win/hack email

o   Answer a question that your ideal reader has or a question widely asked in your niche. Offer a quick hack; e.g., How to grow my email list, How to find my niche, How to set up WordPress, etc.

One email about your struggle

Minimum Viable Blog (MVB)

These are the pages you'll need on your website (if you don't have an existing site and are starting from scratch).

- About page
- Contact page
- Home page
- Work with me page (*If you're a service provider)
- Three posts from your Minimum Viable Content Plan

Case Study 4

Brian is a lawyer who was burnt out and overwhelmed. Although he worked hard, he was always struggling to find new clients every month. He was competing with big firms who have a marketing budget much larger than his. He decided that something had to change, and he started to focus on who he enjoys serving. He realized that he always enjoyed working with online entrepreneurs and he could deliver the best service and expertise with the least amount of effort to this group.

The online business owners he served were also incredibly delighted to work with him. This was the group that gave him the most repeat business and referrals as well. He started to market himself as a lawyer strictly for online entrepreneurs. The number of clients he gets starts to shoot through the roof. He's happier and his clients are happy being served by an expert why understands their needs in detail.

Action Item:

1. Determine who the experts in your niche are. Make a list of the email lists you have to join as well as the blogs you have to follow.

2. What will be your primary content delivery channel?

3. On which social channel(s) will you promote your content?

4. Start brainstorming ideas and fleshing out your content plan, email marketing and blog minimum viable formulas.

CHAPTER 3

CURATE VALUABLE CONTENT THAT POSITIONS YOU AS AN EXPERT

How do you position yourself as an expert by curating content?

A content curator is someone "who continually finds, groups, organizes and shares the best and most relevant content on a specific issue online."[14]

That's what you want to do here.

BECOME A CONTENT CURATOR

If you've started a Twitter account or Facebook business page for your business, you may have heard that you're supposed to share other people's content as well as your own on social media. The acceptable ratio ranges from 50:50, 70:30, or 80:20. You want to curate high-quality content in not just the topic of your expert niche but topics that are complementary as well.

Why?

Because, even if you create a hub of content around your expert niche, there are always content pieces that share a different perspective than yours or that target a different audience but whose strategy or perspective may still be useful for your own audience.

By sharing high-quality content, your audience comes to view you as a trusted and credible source of other complementary topics as well as the ones in your expert niche. They look to you as a conduit to seek other information. You also siphon off some of the street cred of the content that you share because your audience sees that you're keeping up with what's going on in your expert niche.

Mention

Sandra ▪▪▪ ▶ Meera Kothand
May 4 ·

Hi, Meera! I very much enjoy your posts. I've found so many terrific writers as well as blogging and business posts that are very helpful.. thank you!

But how do you know what content to share on social media?

You should curate from a wide range of sources, taking into consideration the following:

- Audience's needs
- Industry news
- Topics that interest you
- Topics that you would write and read about yourself
- Content that sparks conversations

Use tools to help you curate such as Scoop.it!, Pocket, ContentGems, and Twitter Lists. ContentGems and Scoop.it! in particular send a curated list of content links based on the categories that you pick out.

WRITE A ROUNDUP POST

There are two types of roundup posts.

The **first** type curates quotes from several influencers, experts, and bloggers on a particular theme or topic. The bigger and more extensive your roundup is, the higher the chances of that roundup driving huge amounts of traffic to your site. By referring to others, you show your readers that you are familiar with the influencers and micro-influencers in your niche. In essence, this is *borrowing authority* by leveraging their content, which we'll discuss in detail in the next section. Your content automatically becomes more reputable because you're associating yourself with an influencer or micro-influencer in your industry.

When you're asking influencers for a quote, don't forget to "name-drop." Mention that you've already received the nod from another influencer or if you haven't yet, mention the names of influencers you're planning to get a quote from.

See how I've done so in the template below.

Hi, [influencer's first name].

Hope this email finds you well.

My name is <your name> with <your brand>. I wanted to let you know that I've enjoyed reading your blog, and I've learned a lot about <mention specific topics/articles>.

I know you probably get a LOT of emails from people looking for your insight, so I'll keep this really short.

I'm about to publish a new <type of content/blog post/e-book> on <topic> and wanted to know if you'd be willing to share a quote?

You've talked about your experiences on <state topic> before, so I think your quote and thoughts on <topic> will provide a lot of value to readers.

If you'd like to share your thoughts and a quote, I'll add your quote to my <type on content> and share it with you after I publish it on my site.

Just to let you know that <name-drop other micro-influencer> will also be providing her thoughts.

Could you reply with the quote you'd like me to use by <date>?

Thank you so much for your time. Take care.

<Your name>

Here are examples of roundups I have contributed to:

https://solopreneurdiaries.com/social-media-tips-busy-entrepreneurs/

https://sarv.com/resource/post/email-marketing-expert-tips

http://iwannabeablogger.com/first-blog-post/

The **second** type of roundup is a curation of blog posts or content snippets under a similar theme or topic.

An example of this is a post by Erika Madden at Olyvia.co. She features the "best" blog posts by curating them under a single topic: 91+ Outrageously Helpful Blog Posts That Will Make You a Better Blogger + Biz Owner. In this post, she breaks down the posts into categories and highlights the bloggers and influencers who wrote those posts.

Another example is by Raelyn Tan who curated the best tips from 101 different blogging experts by looking through their content: 101 Tips From Top Experts On How To Start A Successful Blog.

These roundup posts take a ton of work and to ensure you get maximum results and exposure, make sure to email each and every blogger and influencer you mentioned in the post.

This accomplishes two things:

a. gets you on the radar of other experts and influencers and helps you build a relationship with them

b. creates a greater chance of your content being shared with a bigger audience through the micro-influencer

Here's an email template you can use.

Hi, [influencer's first name].

Hope things are going well.

I'm <your name> from <your brand>.

I wanted to let you know that I've enjoyed reading your blog and have learned a lot about <mention specific topics/articles>.

I have a new blog post on <enter title>. I mentioned your <blog post/quote> from <blog article source> because <reason why>.

Thank you so much for the work you create and if you have any thoughts or comments on the post, I'd love to know!

<Your name>

Action Item:

1. Sign up for one to two curation tools such as Scoop.it! or ContentGems. Keep a list of sources you regularly want to curate content from.

SECTION III

LEVERAGING THE AUTHORITY ARCHITECTURE

What is authority?

Authority is the ability to get others to listen to you—to be able to impact opinions and purchasing decisions because you have trust and credibility.

You can gain authority by intentionally leveraging what I call the Authority Architecture. This is a three-part framework that allows you to build, borrow, and be the authority. Not everyone in online business has professional qualifications or degrees to showcase. Yet, unspoken rules exist behind who an expert is. In this section, you'll find ideas and strategies you can use to build your own authority architecture. Do you have to implement them all? No, you don't. Pick what aligns best with your strengths and what you are most excited about trying.

CHAPTER 4

BORROW AUTHORITY

When solopreneurs think of authority sites, they think of Entrepreneur, Forbes, or Fast Company. They also think of news and media outlets. But then they remember all the rejections they've heard people receiving from these sites or perhaps the rejections they've faced themselves. They get nervous and anxious and quit even without trying.

It might be your dream to get featured on high-profile sites and podcasts.

But an easier way to work your way up there is to first be featured on smaller sites and podcasts that are within your reach but that still have clout. You're more likely to get noticed by your dream sites if you can name-drop that you were featured on smaller but reputable and recognizable sites and podcasts in your pitches.

You also want to think about connections that will inch you closer to getting featured on your dream sites and podcasts.

For instance, are there writers who post frequently on this site? Where else have they been featured? Who has the owner of the site or podcast worked with? Look at their content or collaborations. Would it be easier to get noticed if you write or get featured on a site that they have a close working relationship with?

HOW TO GET FEATURED ON AUTHORITY SITES AND PODCASTS

Step 1: Build a list of guest posting targets

How do you determine where to guest post or podcast?

1. Is this a site/podcast that your audience frequents?
2. Do they have a similar audience?
3. Does their audience need help with the problems that you solve?

If your answer's a YES, that's a site that's ripe for pitching.

How else can you find suitable guest posts or podcasts?

1. Identify an authority in your space who is a few years ahead of you. Do you have peers who have guest posted or been featured on podcasts before? Where have they done so?

Make a list of 5-10 people who have an overlapping or similar audience to yours and see where they have guest posted. Look at their about pages or home pages for logos or links to external sites. Make a note of these.

Likewise for podcasts, search their names on the iTunes store. All the podcasts they have appeared on will show up. This gives you more podcasts to target. You could also look for new and noteworthy podcasts on the iTunes store. Established businesses are always starting podcasts. Depending on how new they are, they might be on the lookout for guests as well.

2. Use Google in two ways:

- Do a quick search with the following keywords, replacing the word keyword below with the name of your topic
  - Keyword "guest post"
  - Keyword "guest post opportunities"
  - Keyword "guest post guidelines"
  - Keyword "submit guest post"
  - Keyword "guest post"

- Search for aggregated lists on Google
  - Search for "lists of websites that accept guest posts"

3. Go to BuzzSumo and type in your niche as a keyword phrase with quotation marks around it, such as "guest blogging guide" or "guest blogging sites." This will "tell" the sites to search for the exact search phrases within the quotation marks.

Step 2: Eliminate

How recent is the content or podcast?

Is the site active?

You want to eliminate any podcast or site that seems to have stopped producing regular content. For podcasts, you also want to look out for whether the recordings are interviews or solo. This is a good indication of whether the host accepts guests in the first place.

Step 3: Keep a running list of sites and podcasts you want to reach out to

Keep a running list of these sites in a Google Doc.

Include the following information:

- URL
- Link to guest posting guidelines
- Who to send your pitch to—their name and email address

Prioritize this list with a points system

○ How big is the reach of their site?
  Some sites that I use to find data on traffic stats and reach of guest posting sites I target are SimilarWeb and SEMrush. Some people argue that these sites don't give an accurate reflection of the data and that you do have to pay to get their full

suite of services. But this is a good place to get started, and you don't need a paid subscription to get some useful data. You also get to see similar sites that you can potentially target.

Another way to make an estimated guess is by looking at their Twitter handle to see how big their following is. An example points system would be something like this:

Less than 1,000 followers – 1

1,001–5,000 followers – 2

5,001–10,000 followers – 3

10,001–100,000 followers – 4

100,001+ followers– 5

- How likely are you to get your guest post pitch accepted?
  Have a look at their guest posting guidelines. How rigorous are they with the type of content they're expecting? View the other guest posts on their site. What is the quality of the content like? And what type of topics are they looking for?

Are the guest posters newbies or people who are established in their business? Are they open to accepting newbies? Do you think you would be

able to replicate the quality they are looking for?
Use the following points system:

Tier A – Extremely difficult to get pitch accepted –
1
Tier B – Difficult but possible with a good topic – 2
Tier C – Relatively easy to replicate quality as well
as get pitch accepted – 3

Usually, the more difficult it is for your pitch to get
accepted, the more clout the sites likely have and
the more credibility and authority they add to your
name. So I always recommend aiming for Tier B
sites.

- Do you already know the person?
  Is there anyone you know who would be able to link
  you up to them? If so, add 2 points to a site.

This creates a fuss-free ranking system. Tackle the
sites that have more points first and track the
progress of your pitches by the following:
Pitched/Contacted; Booked; Not Successful; Follow
Up. There's a downloadable spreadsheet at
https://nowanexpert.com/bonus.

Step 4: Command attention with a tailor-made guest post or podcast topic

This will vary from site to site.

Look at the most recently published content on their sites as well as the most popular content. Take note of the type of posts and podcasts they usually feature. Are they opinion or strategy-based content, how-to posts, or step-by-step tutorials? Are they question-based podcast interviews or case studies?

How do they start and end their posts and podcasts? Some sites have an extremely short hook that leads into the opening. Others start with a question to the reader. Likewise, some end with a call to action for the reader to comment while others trail off with an open-ended question. How long are the content and recordings?

Now, make a list of topics you can guest post or podcast on.

You know the expert niche you're targeting. What angle can you bring to the table? How can you tailor that information to their audience?

Perhaps their audience are primarily aspiring freelance writers. You're a branding strategist and want to show them the importance of having a writer website and building a brand or platform around their name. That could be a unique guest post that you could write solely for this site.

Step 5: Let them know you exist

Now that you have a list of sites you can target as well as possible topics, do you dive straight into the pitch?

No, you don't because they need to know you exist. A pitch that elicits "Oh, I know this person!" instead of "Who is this person?" makes a whole lot of difference. A warm pitch is always better than a cold pitch. This is why you want to get on the radar of sites you are pitching.

Here are a few ways you can do this:

- **Share their content on social media**

    Make a list of people you want to connect with this year and start showing a genuine interest in their work. I always have a list of content tweets from people I want to connect with. I then set this up to auto loop using IFTTT (I have a tutorial for how you can do this in this post: https://www.meerakothand.com/blog-promotion/).

By sharing their content on my social media profiles, I was able to pitch them guest posts effortlessly because they were familiar with my name. And your goodwill comes back around. Several of them will go the extra mile to retweet and share your posts.

- **Share their work within your content**

Share their work in the form of examples and case studies on your own blog if you have one. This not only boosts your authority as someone who knows your niche well, but it also gives you the opportunity to build goodwill with influencers and micro-influencers. And when they do decide to share your work, it's a huge opportunity to get in front of their fan base. The important step though is to email them and let them know you've linked to one of their posts or resources. In your email, let them know you appreciate their work and share the link to your resource. Here's an example of one of the emails I sent Ramsay from Blog Tyrant.

Hi, Ramsay.

How are you?

I'm Meera, a certified email marketing specialist and freelance writer. I also work with bloggers and solopreneurs on how to craft a strategic online presence at MeeraKothand.com.

I'm a big fan of your work and am one of your list peeps as well.

I just wanted to drop you a note to let you know that I've linked to you in one of my posts. I've included one of your emails as an example of the type of emails bloggers should be sending their list.

Here's a link to the post:

I love your emails, appreciate all that you do, and wanted to let you know.

Take care.

Meera

Did you notice something?

I didn't ask for a share. Influencers are usually so used to getting emails asking them for links, shares, and advice. Of all the influencers I've written to, 80% have shared that piece of content without me even asking. If you'd prefer to ask for a share though, be tactful and tasteful about it.

- **Show off your expertise by commenting on blogs or podcasts you are targeting**

There's nothing radical about blog commenting, but the intention is to put yourself out there and to show that you can make a valuable contribution to the conversation. And you can't do that by posting another "me-too" comment.

The *"great post"* or *"good job"* type of comment.

To be noticed online, your comment has to add to the conversation.

Your comment has to be "head turning."

You also ideally want to be one of the first few to comment on an influencer's site. At times, by the time you make it to a popular blogger's site to read their post, there are over thirty comments and you wonder if it really matters if you comment. Because you're not going to have anything to add to the conversation since the thirty people before you have already done so.

Here's how you can get in on the action when the post is still fresh. I do most of my blog reading from Feedly. On Feedly, I created a separate category of all the bloggers I'd like to connect with. Then in IFTTT, I run the recipe below. IFTTT is a free web-based service that connects different applications through recipes.

Get new articles emailed to you from Feedly.

What this does is send me an automatic email notification when there is a new blog post from one of the blogs in my chosen category.

But that doesn't mean I comment on all the posts I get a notification for. I only comment if I can *add* to the conversation and it's a topic I genuinely am interested in. Remember the three content levers that signify what it means to *add*? Take note of those as you write your comment.

Step 6: The Pitch

A pitch isn't a scary email. There's nothing complicated about it. I've embedded a few sample pitch templates I've used and still use today.

PITCH TEMPLATE 1: USED FOR COLD PITCHES

Hi, [first name of editor].

I know you get a lot of emails from people looking for your insight, so I'll keep this short.

I'm [your name] with [your brand]. I love the content on your site and always refer to it when I'm looking for advice about [topic].

I've been published on [state which sites with a link back to the article]. I would love the opportunity to be able to contribute to the [name of site you're pitching] community as well.

I have an idea for a guest post that your readers will find interesting. The topic I'd like to propose is [state title of topic].

In this post, [give a gist of the topic and the subheads].

As per your submission guidelines, I have provided the [state what you are attaching with the email or document; e.g., Google Docs link, pic attachment, or alternative headlines].

This post will dive deeper into the topic of [state topic] and complement these two other posts on your site.

[Links to site]

I hope you'll find this to be a good fit for the site. Thank you so much for your time and consideration.

[Your name]

[Professional signature at bottom of email]

PITCH TEMPLATE 2: USED FOR WARM PITCHES WHEN THEY ARE FAMILIAR WITH YOUR NAME

Hi, [first name of editor].

How are you doing?

I hope my name rings a bell. We've connected on Twitter and in your blog comments several times. I'm a huge fan of your work and as you know, regularly share your posts because they are super detailed.

I've been contributing guest posts to several communities like [include names of sites you've been featured] and would love the opportunity to contribute to the [name of host's] community as well.

I wanted to check if you are open to considering a guest post on one of the topics below?

[Include topic titles and subheads or bullet points]

For both topics, I will give screenshots with examples from other sites. I'll also propose alternative headlines for the chosen topic.

I hope you'll find the topics to be a good fit for [name of community]. Do let me know what you think.

Thank you so much.

[Professional signature at bottom of email]

PITCH TEMPLATE 3: WARM PODCAST PITCH

Hi, [first name of podcast host].

I'm a huge fan of your podcasts, and your show has helped a ton with my business. I've been recommending that several of my friends listen in to your show, and I've left a review on iTunes as well.

I'm [your name] with [your brand].

I've been published on [state which sites with a link back to the article] and have also been on several of these shows [links to shows]. I was listening to the last two podcast episodes and had a couple of ideas about [state topic]. They would really complement these episodes that you did [links to episodes].

Here are a few ideas I came up with for your audience:

1.
2.
3.

I love sharing more about [state topic] because [how is it helpful for their audience]. I'd love to know if you'd be keen on chatting about this on your show?

And, of course, I'd love to promote this podcast to my own audience. I can send a solo email to my email list of [number on email list] and promote it on social media. I currently have [Twitter followers], [Facebook fans], [Facebook group members], and [LinkedIn connections].

If you have a calendar link, I'd be happy to find a time that works for both of us to chat. Just in case, here's my own calendar link [calendar link].

You can reach me any time at [email address]. My Skype ID is [Skype ID], and you can also find me at [link to your site].

Thank you so much for reading through my information. I look forward to connecting soon!

[Professional signature at bottom of email]

PITCH NO-NO'S

Your pitch might be the first impression someone forms about you, so make it count. Recently, I have been on the receiving end of several pitches and here are the mistakes I see.

There is no introduction of who you are or where the host can find your content

- You don't have to be an expert. But you do need to state the niche you're in and what you write about. Links to other posts or articles would help as well.

What topics are you suggesting and why would they be a good fit?

- Research the host's site thoroughly before sending in a pitch so that they don't feel like you haven't considered their audience at all. Imagine getting a fitness article pitch for a digital marketing blog.

You're not familiar with the host's work

- You don't have to fake being in love with the host's work but some recognition that you have actually looked around on the site and are familiar with their content is a plus point. Would your post complement another existing article on the site? That's a bonus and the host would love to know that.

You ask the host to give you ideas on what you should write about

- I've had discussions with several of the sites I've guest posted for on what topic would be a good fit for their editorial calendar, but it always has to start with a proposal from you. Make an effort to come up with topics and do some research on them.

You don't read the guidelines

- Most hosts have a clear link to guest posting or podcast interview guidelines on their contact page or footer. Make an effort to click around the site before reaching out with an email asking if they're taking guests.

You disappear once the guest post is published

- When you *do* guest post, be thankful and

respectful. The host has lent you the platform that they've built. When people take the time to leave a comment, reply to every single one even if the host responds to the comment. It's a nice gesture and gives you an opportunity to build a relationship with the host. Don't disappear once the post is published.

Step 7: Position your guest post or podcast interview for success

Once you're successfully featured on a guest post or podcast, you can ramp up your credibility and authority by showcasing the logo of the guest post or podcast you just got featured on. But there's more you can do to optimize this opportunity. You want to capture some of your host's traffic back to your own site. But you don't stop there. You want to convert that traffic to subscribers. There are a few ways you can do this.

- **Craft your author bio and be strategic about it**

The author bio is your tiny piece of real estate for adding value to the host's site. Don't stuff your author bio with 4-5 links of all your social media profiles.

Give people too many choices and they take none. At the most, provide links to one social media profile and one landing page. Here's an example of an author bio I've written. There's just one single link that heads straight to a landing page.

> About the Author: Meera is a freelance writer and tad bit of a nerd who loves supporting busy solopreneurs and bloggers find focus, build authority & stand out online. Struggling with what to write or send your email list? Steal her Swipe File of 2 years worth of content hacks for emails & blog posts. Download it here.

But here's where you can go the extra step. Rather than sending people to your home page, which most likely has more than one call to action, you can send them to a custom landing page.

- **Create a custom landing page for their audience**

If your host has a name for his or her tribe, call out to them in the header of your landing page. Readers have clicked through from the host's site, and this creates a sense of familiarity. Here's an example of a custom landing page where I did just that.

Tie that landing page to an opt-in incentive that's linked to the content you just delivered. For one of the guest posts I did, I potentially lost out on hundreds of subscribers because I didn't create an opt-in incentive that was aligned with the guest post content I wrote before it went live.

- **Create short links (bonus points if they're branded) to custom landing pages prior to your podcast interview.**

In a podcast interview, the host will likely ask you where someone can find you or learn more about the topic you just spoke about. Imagine if I rattled off the link meerakothand.com/send-email-list versus if I said meera.email/course or meera.tips/content?

The second set will obviously stick better in the minds of listeners. Here's how you can do that:

- Use a branded short link provider such as Rebrandly or SHORT.cm. Both have free plans which allow at least one branded URL to be used. You can purchase domains from as low as $2.88 a year from Namecheap to use for your branded short links.

  Some examples you can try are [yourbizname].tips, [yourbizname].support, or [yourbizname].email.

- Alternatively, simply use a link shortener like bit.ly or TinyURL.

If your short link goes directly to a landing page, you'll have a higher chance of converting this traffic to subscribers. This is where that middle of funnel content we spoke about in the previous section comes in handy. If you have your Minimum Viable Email Marketing in place, you will nurture these new subscribers on auto rather than worry about what to send them as you see your list grow. See how everything clicks and links together?

Action Item:

1. What can you do to borrow authority? Create a list of sites you can reach out to and go through the points system to rank them.

2. Create a system to get on their radar through commenting or sharing their work.

CHAPTER 5

BUILD AUTHORITY

The best way to build authority is when you display your expertise. Content, which we discussed in the previous section, is a huge component of building authority. In this chapter, you'll discover a few other ideas that'll help you build authority.

RUN A FREE CHALLENGE(S) TO SOLVE A SPECIFIC PROBLEM IN YOUR EXPERT NICHE

Challenges are short bursts of activity tied to a promise or outcome that you're helping your audience attain. They usually run for 3–7 days and consist of daily emails with supplementary material. Many challenges are tied to a pop-up Facebook group or community where you can provide support for challenge participants.

While challenges do take time and effort to set up, they help you fast track your path to building authority because you're helping participants achieve a specific desired outcome or helping them find answers to a problem in a short span of time.

If you add a video component, either in the material you deliver daily or when you show up live in the pop-up Facebook group, you also help to amp up your KNOW-LIKE-TRUST factor. Here are the steps you need to take to deliver a challenge.

Step 1: Decide on the goal of your challenge

The goal of your challenge is important because it'll help you determine how much content you need to execute the challenge. Many solopreneurs use challenges as an event before they open the cart to a product or service they are launching. But challenges can also be used to grow your email list or establish your authority in an area.

Step 2: Decide who this challenge is for and where you will promote it

Who are you targeting with this challenge?

Are there ads that you can run for a short period of time?

Do you have peers with an audience you can reach out to, or who can share your challenge?

Are there Facebook groups you can share the challenge in?

Step 3: What results can they expect after completing your challenge?

What do you want your audience to get out of the challenge? What is one quick win or one promise that you can deliver?

Step 4: Decide on the length of your challenge

You want to overdeliver on your challenge content but be wary of the number of days you run your challenge for. Longer challenges have a higher dropout rate. Even with a 5-day challenge, you have an attrition rate as you enter the 4th and 5th days. So try to keep your challenge to 5–7 days so that your audience doesn't tire out. You also want to keep them looking forward to each day of content you release.

Step 5: Pick your challenge title

Here are a few challenge title templates you can use.

a. _____?

   (problem/challenge/struggle)

A 7-day challenge for you to _____

   (big promise/solution/desire)

E.g., Struggling to lose the weight even with diet and exercise? Take part in this 7-day challenge to lose 5 pounds without going hungry or feeling miserable

b. _____ Challenge

   (name/main subject)

_____ in just _____

   (result)   (time frame) (tool/method)

E.g., Transform your living room 5-day challenge. Get the house of your dreams in just 60 minutes a day using my XYZ method

c. _____ Challenge

   (name, result driven)

In 5 Days Learn How to Get_____

(desired results)

Through/By Using _____

(method/tool)

E.g., "Yousave" Challenge where you save 60 minutes every day.

In 5 days learn how to save 60 precious minutes of your workday by using the power of XYZ

d. _____ Challenge:

(name)

Get _____ in 7 Days

(result/promise)

Receive_____ to

(tool/method)

_____

(result/a promise)

E.g., Gain 100 Followers in 7 Days. Receive a daily action plan to seriously boost your following on Twitter!

Step 6: Create promotional content

Make promotional images as you would for your other content. If you're creating a pop-up Facebook group, include the name of the challenge as well as your image to show them who the group is hosted by. If you're doing a video, I highly suggest going live on the first and last days or first day and mid-challenge.

Remember you are trying to get them to associate you with this topic of expertise so that you can build authority. Here are some examples of promotional content I used when I hosted my email marketing challenge.

Step 7: Create your critical pages and content

Here are the critical pages you need to set up for your challenge and the steps you need to take.

- A landing page to get sign-ups for your challenge
- A thank you page to redirect them to after they sign up
- On your thank you page, you can ask them to share the challenge and remind them to click confirm on the confirmation email.
- A confirmation page

- After they have clicked confirm on your email, link to your pop-up Facebook group on your confirmation page and remind them about the start date of the challenge.
- Send an email to welcome them to the challenge.
- Create your challenge supporting material as well as daily prompts you will use in your pop-up Facebook group. The prompts are meant to boost engagement and get them to ask questions. You want to interact with and be heavily involved in your challenge group and answer as many questions as you can.

CREATE INTERACTIVE CONTENT

Interactive content is a chance for you to prove your expertise live. It allows your audience to interact with your content in a way that's highly personalized or watch you give a transformative experience to someone similar to them via your expertise.

Live coaching or live transformations

Examples of interactive content are hot seat sessions or live coaching and transformations.

Are you a brand strategist? Show your audience live the elements on their site that are not working for their brand. If you're a coach, do a coaching session on camera with your audience. Hot seat sessions where you can do live coaching and give your ideal audience a quick transformation are perfect examples of interactive content.

Quizzes and assessments

Quizzes and assessments are other types of interactive content. A quiz, like any marketing asset or content, should have a purpose and be specific. It has to align with your expert business and the products or services you offer or intend to offer. As an expert, you want to attract people struggling with a particular issue. Your quiz can work as a diagnostic tool, telling people *what* they struggle with and *how* to fix it.

For instance, if I'm interested in attracting people struggling with email marketing, my quiz could be on "let's pick your opt-in incentive" or "email marketing readiness quiz." Their answers to the quiz tell me what stage they're at and allow me to segment them based on their struggles. I can then send them targeted emails depending on what their results were. You need to determine what outcomes people will gain from taking your quiz and where you are leading them to. You could deliver the results in a PDF with action steps or follow up with an email sequence.

CONSIDER USING HARO (HELP A REPORTER OUT)

If you're looking for opportunities to be quoted in articles or print, HARO is a simple way to get connected with journalists. This daily newsletter lists topics and stories where a reporter is looking for someone with a particular expertise or skill set. Every time your name and your business appear in print is an opportunity to attract new readers and further establishes you as an expert in that niche topic.

SELF-PUBLISH YOUR OWN BOOK

Several people suggest writing a book as a way to build authority. A book certainly helps with building authority, but it's a time-intensive activity and isn't the most cost-effective option for a person just starting out.

Why?

Self-publishing books costs money. You would need to hire a designer for your book cover. You would need to pay for the formatting and editing of those books too. If you don't want your book to just sit on a digital bookshelf collecting dust and you want to get it in as many hands as possible, you would also need to pay for promotion. Otherwise, your book won't have a fighting chance of being ranked in Amazon's competitive categories.

So if self-publishing is a means to an end—growing your email list or building authority—I highly suggest starting with the other strategies before turning to self-publishing your own books.

Action Item:

1. What can you do to build authority? List strategies that you are excited about trying, and those that you can implement quickly.

SECTION IV

MARKETING YOUR EXPERTISE

"I love creating content, but I seriously suck at marketing. I always feel shy when I need to market because I'm scared of being too salesy."

These were the words a subscriber sent me recently.

Does that sound anything like you?

You hate marketing for fear of sounding too salesy.

You wish you could grow your online business without having to market yourself or your products.

Ever felt that way?

I have, till I realized that everything I was doing was marketing.

Whether you like it or not, as long as you're in some form of business (quick definition: where goods and services are exchanged for one another or for money), you're engaged in marketing.

Marketing boils down to a simple formula:

Attract > Capture > Engage > Convert

If you break these down, your marketing system has these six parts:

- Identify your target audience
- Attract them to your site
- Capture your target audience
- Nurture that target audience
- Convert them to buyers
- Turn them into brand advocates or repeat customers

So if your business activity falls into any of these six areas, you're doing some form of marketing.

Marketing doesn't have to be about blowing your own trumpet. There are several subtle ways that you can market yourself and build your credibility as an expert. Because being seen as an expert is as much about your social proof and visibility as it is about the depth of knowledge you have.

In this section, you'll discover simple but highly effective ways of boosting credibility via social proof and visibility markers. You'll also discover systems and reusable marketing assets you need to have to build an expert-based business.

CHAPTER 6

SOCIAL PROOF & CREDIBILITY
FAST TRACK

When you're new to business, you don't have testimonials in the dozens to pick from. You haven't sold tens or hundreds of your e-books or courses either. Your email list could just be slowly starting to take off. Yet, you need to be able to get people to pay attention to you.

You need to convince them to sign up to your email list. Convince them to not bounce away and spend more than a couple of seconds reading your content. And you need to give them the confidence that you are indeed capable of helping them.

That's what having influence is about. Influence is "the capacity to have an effect on the character, development, or behavior of someone or something."[15]

In the best-selling book *Influence*,[16] Robert Cialdini states that reciprocity, commitment & consistency, social proof, authority, liking, and scarcity are strategies to build influence.

In this section, you'll discover suggestions to boost your digital presence, increase your conversions, lift your reputation as an expert in your niche, and command the attention you deserve. Many of these suggestions are based on the principles that Cialdini mentioned and how they relate to building an expert business online.

PRIME YOUR DIGITAL PRESENCE

A subpar digital presence does nothing to boost your standing as an expert. There are several tiny elements about your digital presence that give people the impression of whether you're the go-to expert or not.

What do people see when they google you?

How do you appear on Google Search? Is it immediately clear what you do and who you help serve? When you google your name, does your website appear at the top of Google's search results?

Here are screenshots of two other entrepreneurs and how they appear on the Google Search feed. As you can see, it's evident at a glance what type of business they have as well as who they help serve. If you have the Yoast plug-in, it's really simple to "tell" Google how you want to appear on the search feed.

Becky Mollenkamp, a Business Coach for Women Entrepreneurs
https://beckymollenkamp.com/ ▼
Becky Mollenkamp is a business coach for women entrepreneurs. She helps women navigate the mindset and tactical struggles of self-employment.

Jessica Stansberry
jessicastansberry.com/ ▼
Infopreneur and systems guru for online business owners.
How to Create an Interactive ... · The blog · Meet me · Copy My Trello Boards

2. Can they connect you to your area of expertise?

Let's say your website does appear at the top of Google's search results, but what happens after they click through to your site? Studies have found that visitors only spend a few seconds[17] assessing your website before deciding whether to stay or leave. Within five seconds,[18] will your ideal customer be able to tell what you do, what problem you solve for your readers, as well as why they should choose you?

What they want to know is: *What's in it for me?*

An ideal place to reveal what you are an expert in and how you help people is on the header of your website.

In *StoryBrand,*[20] Donald Miller suggests a four-part one-liner statement. The statement would include (1) the character (who you are helping), (2) the problem (that you're helping to solve), (3) the plan (how are you going to help them) and, (4) the success (what's the outcome).

Another way of looking at it is simply: What you do – Who you help – Your benefit

Here are some examples of people who have done this.

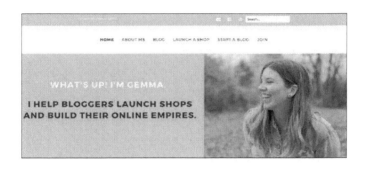

3. Do all your social media accounts have the same branded look and feel?

It's important to communicate a singular brand identity right through every channel of communication and connection with your audience. You can do this by having social media headers with the same look and feel as well as a consistent profile right through to help you establish and build on your brand equity.

4. Can they put a face to the name?

If you're already commenting on other blogs and forums, you've noticed that some commenters appear as an unknown avatar like this one below.

Kristen W · 3 months ago

Hi Meera! Thank you for this post-- packed with great information. A follow up question. How do you best evaluate what a pain point for your audience is, that you can then turn into a product to service. Second question-- do you think your audience needs to be a certain size to sell to-- or have a certain size subscription list?

Maybe yours does.

Blog comment systems like DISQUS require you to log in via Facebook or Twitter and your image gets pulled from these accounts. But other comment systems pull your image off Gravatar. So if you don't have an image on Gravatar, you're not going to be recognized as the face of your brand no matter how valuable your comment is.

It's very easy to set this up, and I recommend doing this before you start commenting on others' sites.

• Go to Gravatar.com

- Sign up for a WordPress account if you don't already have one. Or log in with the same email and password you use for your WordPress site.
- Verify your email address and account.
- Click on Add Image to upload your Gravatar photo. For consistency, use the same picture across social media.
- Assign the new photo to be your Gravatar. You also have the option of assigning different profile pictures for different email addresses using the same account.

5. Do you have a professional email address?

If you want to look professional, get an email address that includes your domain name: for example, name@yourdomain.com. G Suite offers this for $5 a month, and they even help you run through the set-up over the phone.

6. Can they find your business Facebook page through your personal profile?

If you're interacting in Facebook groups, give people a chance to find out about your business via your profile page. Add your business Facebook page to your personal profile and make sure a link to your website is clearly visible on your profile page.

Now, let's dive deeper into elements that will fast track your influence even if you're brand new, by applying Cialdini's principles.

1. Become relatable and likable

People do business or follow people whom they can relate to or like. If you're building an expert business, you want to place your picture front and center on the header of your website, on your side bar, as well as on your about page. This helps your audience connect with you and put a face to your brand. So ditch the stock image for an image of yourself with a "what you do" statement. The photo you use should also be aligned with how your brand is perceived. Or if you're starting out, how you want your brand to be perceived. See how Mary Fernandez of Persuasion Nation and Trena Little have done this on their sites.

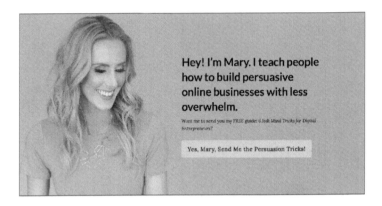

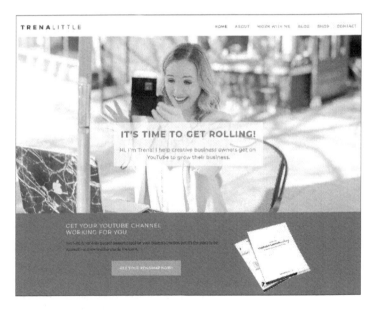

2. Encourage reciprocity by offering a free lead magnet (or opt-in incentive) that's related to your expertise and business model

The easiest way to encourage reciprocity is to offer an opt-in incentive or lead magnet. This is a piece of content that you give away for free to your subscribers in exchange for their email address. Your lead magnet is the one that gets your reader in the door and converts them to a subscriber and later on, potentially a buyer. It's the first step in building a relationship with your reader.

If you offer services or coaching, what will make it easy for them to take the first step and try out your service/coaching? What burning questions do you need to answer before they sign up for your packages?

If you offer digital products, you want to give them a quick takeaway so that you gain their trust.

If you're a physical product creator, what can you offer that will help them quickly make their first purchase? If they're in the market for your product, what will help them make an informed buying decision?

127

What you offer as an incentive has to be aligned with the problem your expert niche is trying to solve as well as your business model.

3. Leverage herd mentality or fear of missing out with social proof

If this many people have listened to this podcast, are in this Facebook group, have taken this course, or have downloaded this guide, it has to be good, right?

Something about the power of numbers stirs people to take action because they don't want to be at the losing end.

Note: You don't have to have a huge email list or follower numbers in the millions to use this method. A hack to get around this is to use the sum of all followers on all your social media channels and your email subscribers.

Here are some ways you can present this:

- X entrepreneurs are already [describe the benefit] using [your opt-in offer]. Add your email address below and be the next one.

E.g., 1,000 designers have already doubled their monthly earnings using our exclusive guide. Simply enter your email address below and be the next one.

If you do have results to share, present them on your opt-in forms or headers:

- I [what did you achieve]. Want to know how I did it? Subscribe below.

  E.g., I got completely booked out within two months of launching my business—and you can too. Want to know how I did it? Subscribe below.

See how Raelyn Tan does it on her site.

Join 8,000 others and sign up for my Free 7-day Turbo Your Blog Traffic + Email List Mini Course.

Can't grow your business because you have no audience to speak of? Don't know how to grow your email list?

Learn how to get more traffic and subscribers for your blog + business with 7 days of proven visibility strategies. Sign up now! (it's free)

I WANT MORE TRAFFIC & SUBSCRIBERS »

4. Enhance your authority by showing authority markers or "as seen in" logos

The earlier section on authority architecture gave you several steps to follow if you want to leverage and borrow others' platforms. If you followed through on those steps and spoke at a summit or on a podcast or guest posted on a well-known site, featuring the logo of the site is a simple but highly effective way to boost your credibility. Prime locations to feature logos are just below your site header and on your home page.

See how Dana Malstaff at Boss Mom has done this on her site.

See how I've done this on my website too.

5. Invite commitment

If you've read my book *Your First 100*, you'll be familiar with the term micro-commitments. These are tiny actions that you get your ideal customer to make, e.g., follow you on social media, sign up to your email list, or watch a video. Your audience needs to get used to you asking them to take tiny steps or actions. These tiny actions pave the way to bigger things and will get them to see you as an authority as well as someone they will go on to do business with.

You can combine several of the elements above to boost your social proof and credibility.

See how Bailey Richert does it on her site. She has two elements of social proof. She invites the reader to join thousands of others who are learning what she teaches. She also includes logos of sites where she has been featured.

CHAPTER 6A

MINIMUM VIABLE MARKETING FORMULA (PART 2)

Minimum Viable Social Media and Visibility Plan

Many solopreneurs believe that to achieve this idea of being everywhere, they need to get on every social media platform available. This actually works in reverse and doesn't allow you to make a mark on any one platform. This is where the Minimum Viable Social Media and Visibility Plan comes into play.

- Claim profile name on pertinent social media platforms (LinkedIn, Instagram, Pinterest, Facebook, etc.)
- Choose two social media platforms depending on your goals and where your target audience are most likely to hang out on.

- If your aim is to focus heavily on borrowing authority via guest posts and podcasts, you might want to consider Twitter as a channel to connect with other influencers and experts.

- Create social media images to promote opt-in incentive created under the Minimum Viable Email Marketing (MVEM) umbrella on the chosen social media platforms.

- Create social media images for each blog post created under the Minimum Viable Blog (MVB).

- Set up your Gravatar image.

- Identify five micro-influencers. Comment on influencer's posts/share their work.

- Approach these micro-influencers about guest posting on their blogs.

Action Item:

1. Pick one to two elements that you can add in the next few days to boost credibility and social proof.

2. Implement your Minimum Viable Social Media and Visibility Plan.

CHAPTER 7

INCORPORATING SET AND FORGET MARKETING SYSTEMS AND REUSABLE MARKETING ASSETS

Marketing assets are materials such as emails, PDFs, videos, infographics, quizzes, or audio files that help you with any or all of the six different phases of marketing that we discussed at the start of the section. The type of asset you use will be based on the goal of the marketing campaigns or plans that you run. Marketing assets can be reused, but they should also be reviewed regularly to ensure that they are up to date and still relevant.

Here are some examples of marketing assets that you can reuse in your business.

- A set of prewritten emails in an autoresponder that are sent out to all new subscribers regardless of when they join your email list. This is an important aspect of your nurture funnel. You can easily get started here by using the suggested sequence in Minimum Viable Email Marketing.

- Canned email responses to questions you get asked about most

- A welcome onboarding email series sent out to new clients or buyers showing them how to contact you, what the support avenues are (e.g., Slack, Facebook group, Voxer), how to access their learning material as well as where and how they should book their calls if they haven't done so

- A pre-welcome questionnaire or video for potential clients to learn about your process as well as the steps they'll take if they decide to work with you

- Specific lead magnets that lead into each of your offers

Systems help you set up processes to automate marketing so that they can repeat themselves time and again with little to no extra effort.

Automation is not scheduling. In fact, it's the very opposite. Scheduling is manually batching an area of work so that it can be published or shared later. Queuing your posts in WordPress to be published later, loading your Buffer queue, and loading your pictures on Grum are examples of scheduling.

The following are mainstay systems that are most useful for beginner small business owners and solopreneurs trying to build an expert-based business.

- A lead capture system integrated with your email marketing system. These could be opt-in forms, landing pages, top bars, or exit intent pop-ups that capture website visitors' email addresses and deliver your lead magnet to them on auto. Examples of lead capture systems are those offered by Thrive Landing Pages and Thrive Leads, Leadpages, or OptinMonster. There are several options in the market, and you should pick one based on the price point you are comfortable with, whether it's a one-time or recurring fee, features, and ease of use.

- An email marketing system that allows you to create automated sequences for each specific group or core opt-in incentive. There are several email service providers in the market that provide drip email functionality at various price points. The more popular options for solopreneurs are ConvertKit, ActiveCampaign, MailChimp or MailerLite.

- A tool for potential clients to book meetings or calls with you. Skype or Zoom are popular choices.

- A calendar or scheduling tool for potential clients to book meetings with you. Calendly or Acuity Scheduling are popular choices.

- A content scheduling tool like Buffer or MeetEdgar so that you can drip curated content out on social media.

- A Welcome onboarding sequence of emails for new clients or new customers.

- A storage place such as Google Drive or Dropbox to store opt-in incentives and to share files.

- Need clients to fill in a survey or questionnaire before your call? Use Zapier to have this sent out on auto.

By using reusable marketing assets as well as systems, you are investing time up-front just once in order to deliver timely service and a better experience for your audience repeatedly with little to no extra effort.

If you are looking for a way to review your digital presence, marketing assets, and systems, you may want to consider the *CREATE: Intensive Workbook and Planner for Solopreneurs* at createplanner.com

Action Item:

1. What systems or assets is your expert business in urgent need of? Make a list of them.

SECTION V

BUILDING A MARKETING CAMPAIGN

You have a slew of strategies on building your expert business from scratch. But how do you start implementing these and in what order? This section will help you translate what you have been reading into real, tangible steps that you will take to build your credibility and authority as an expert. And it all starts with building a marketing campaign.

Marketing campaigns have one specific goal that is usually for a predetermined amount of time. There are several different types of campaigns with the most popular ones being brand awareness or brand-building campaigns and sales campaigns.

Brand awareness campaigns are a series of steps designed to introduce your brand to the world and increase awareness about the work you do to an audience. Most of the goals or calls to action surrounding these campaigns are lead generation based; e.g., sign-ups for an opt-in incentive that solves a specific problem in your expert niche, click-throughs to posts that address a popular problem in the topic of your expert niche in a bid to capture that traffic on to your email list. Some other examples of brand-building campaign goals are to increase social media followers or Facebook fan page likes. Sales campaigns are a series of steps designed to introduce an offer and sell it to a specific audience. Most of the goals or calls to action surrounding these campaigns are number of sales, number of people enrolled, or number of pre-orders and bookings.

In this case, our goal is brand awareness—to establish your authority as an expert in your niche. In this section, you'll work out your 180-day marketing plan based on the strategies you've discovered in this book. We'll also discuss different types of metrics to gauge the success of your content.

CHAPTER 8

CREATE YOUR MARKETING PLAN

For your marketing plan to work, you need to reverse engineer the process starting with the outcome you want. If you have a pen and empty notebook, grab them before you go through these questions. Alternatively, download the printable worksheet at **https://nowanexpert.com/bonus.**

1. What niche do you want to become the go-to expert in?

2. What's your goal?
I.e., to become the go-to expert for _____ within _____

3. What milestones do you have?

These should be measurable and if achieved, will help you realize your goal. E.g., I will be asked to speak at an industry conference, I will have ten full-time clients in my portfolio within eight months, I will become a contributor on Forbes, etc.

4. Why is this important to you?

5. Plan your **180-Day Marketing Push** Activities

- What is your start date?
- What is your end date? (In this case, an end date is arbitrary because you have to continuously take steps to build upon your expert status so that you can attract and nurture more people. But an end date would be a good gauge for you to take stock of what you did and what you can change going forward.)
- What content pieces will you incorporate? This is where you implement your Minimum Viable Content Plan.
- Do you have a site and do you intend to incorporate a blog as part of your site? If so, implement the Minimum Viable Blog.

- What marketing assets do you need? Minimally you will need a lead magnet and a welcome email series.

- What strategies will you use to **borrow** authority? List all the methods you will use and the sites you intend to pitch.

- What strategies will you use to **build** authority? List all the methods you will use.

- What systems do you need? Minimally you will need a lead capture system and an autoresponder. You also need to implement your Minimum Viable Email Marketing Plan, which includes a welcome email or welcome email series for new subscribers.

- What tweaks or changes do you need to implement or incorporate to boost your digital presence and credibility? This is where you implement your Minimum Viable Social Media and Visibility Plan.

6. Put your plan into a marketing calendar

Now that you have a plan of what you want to do, you need to put it down on your marketing calendar and organize it according to what you need to accomplish each month. Build out your minimum viable plans first before moving on to work on the rest.

This isn't complicated in any way. You take everything you have sketched out in your 180-Day Marketing Push and break it out into months. Here's an example of what Months 1 – 3 may look like. Flesh this out for the next six months and get as specific as you can about when you'll carry out these activities.

I have a sample marketing plan you can download at **https://nowanexpert.com/bonus.**

Month 1

What content will you create: Implement MV Content Plan. Plot out specific days you will do writing and publishing.

On which channels will you promote your content: Twitter, Pinterest, etc.

Create Minimum Viable Blog pages (About, Contact, Home).

Prepare a list of sites to pitch and rank them using the points system.

Start piecing together Minimum Viable Email Marketing (MVEM).

Month 2

Authority-building activities: Start sharing content from micro-influencers & influencers in pitch plan. Pitch minimum of two sites/podcasts a week. Specify the sites and the days you will do the pitching.

What content will you create: Implement MV Content Plan. Plot out specific days you will do writing and publishing.

What marketing assets will you create: Promotional images to promote content pieces & opt-in incentive on chosen social media platforms, content upgrade for three posts.

Social proof + credibility: Request testimonials/feedback at the end of welcome email series.

Work out content and email editorial calendar for three months.

Month 3

Authority-building activities: Pitch minimum two sites a week. Specify the sites and the days you will do the pitching.

What content will you create: Batch write two posts for your own content medium.

What marketing assets will you create: Free email course, visuals to promote email course, etc.

Social proof + credibility: Update home page with testimonial, replace header stock image with head shot and "what I do statement," add top bar to optimize site.

7. How will you measure results?

Most content metrics fall into the following five groups.

Lead generation metrics: number of leads, conversions, etc.

User behavior: page views, bounce rate, session duration, etc.

Engagement metrics: likes, shares, comments, mentions, etc.

SEO metrics: organic traffic, backlinks, keyword rankings, dwell time, etc.

Sales metrics: direct sales, ROI, etc.

In this case, you know the goal of your marketing campaign. But how will you know if your campaign is successful? Are you looking to monitor awareness through word-of-mouth marketing or website visits? Are you also looking to grow and nurture your email list? What numbers will you track in order to analyze whether what you're doing is working?

Don't forget to track the amount of time and effort each activity took as well. Did the podcast you were featured on get you more subscribers and website visits than your guest posts? Did you notice that the time and effort spent on events like summits exceeds the impact or results? This is how you'll measure ROI in the future.

By fleshing out your marketing plan in this way you know what you have to do and why. Every activity you write down on your marketing plan has a purpose.

Seem like a lot of work?

It is.

Your minimum viable marketing plans are necessities for building a strong business foundation, so there's no escaping those. And once you have the planning out of the way and a task gets on your calendar, it gets done. This is the quickest way to start paving the way to becoming a go-to expert in your niche.

CHAPTER 9

HOW NOT TO BECOME ANOTHER ME-TOO EXPERT

You already know about the steps you need to take to establish expert status in your niche.

But what if the niche you picked is still saturated?

"Experts" are a dime a dozen. You don't want to be another me-too expert. Unless you can create a powerful and distinct difference to your audience, you will appear to have the same product or service as everyone else. You will appear to have nothing new to offer them that the others already don't.

There are five different ways that experts can differentiate themselves:

- Marketing
- Content
- Process
- Relationship
- Customer Experience

Marketing

Remember that marketing refers to any of the following six activities:

- Identifying your target audience
- Attracting them to your site
- Capturing your target audience
- Nurturing that target audience
- Converting them to buyers
- Turning them into brand advocates or repeat customers

How are your competitors approaching each of these activities? Does anything set them apart? How can *you* set yourself apart?

Content

What content mediums do they use? What do you

think their strengths are? Are there any content mediums that you could leverage?

Process

Do they claim to have a style or process of solving problems in your niche? What is their method and how is it different? What promise do they make to their audience? Have a look at their home page and about page.

Relationship

Do they enjoy word-of-mouth marketing? What does their audience say about them? Look at the comments they get on their content. Listen in on the social conversation to glean some of these insights.

Where will you stake your claim? This is where it's useful to do a competitor audit to see where each of them stands with regard to the above five elements. Here are some ways you can do this research:

- Sign up for the email lists of your competitors and niche market.
- Read the websites and blogs of your competitors.

- Follow businesses and individuals from your niche market on social media to see the type of content they are curating.

Customer Experience

Do they provide a good overall experience? In my book *Your First 100*, I mention the 5P Touch Framework and the importance of a holistic experience to create repeat, loyal customers.

These are as follows:

- **Pre**-Touch Point is where your ideal customers have not directly interacted with you yet and have only heard of your brand from external sources.
- **Premier (First)** Touch Point defines their first interaction with you or your brand.
- **Pivotal** Touch Point is where you engage with your ideal customers and show them that you understand their pain points.
- **Prime** Touch Point is the interaction just before a sale where you help them to overcome their objections and support them through the buying process.

- **Post** Touch Point refers to the after-sales support your customers receive and how much your brand delights them post-purchase.
- Are your competitors leveraging all five touch points? What aren't they doing or what could they do better?

Fill in the information in a simple table like this. This is how you can start thinking about how you can make doing business with you irresistible.

Other Experts in Your Niche	Customer Experience	Marketing	Content	Process	Relationship

CONCLUSION + NEXT STEPS

You now have everything you need to start building your brand as the go-to expert for your identified niche.

But becoming an expert is not somewhere you arrive at.

It's a commitment to a niche or topic—a commitment to sharing about that topic with your audience. You also want to differentiate yourself in the minds of your ideal customers.

Commitment and differentiation are the two key ingredients.

The online business environment changes rapidly. The things your ideal audience are interested in may also shift. You have to keep current and continuously learn and apply your knowledge and skills. Here are some tips as you navigate and establish your expert-based business.

Work on having a "worldview" rather than an original idea

Nothing is original.

All creative work builds on what came before. How you circumvent this is by being YOU. You bring a unique mix of experiences, skills, and the magic of your personal worldview. A worldview is a filter or a lens through which you see the world. It determines how you see people, brands, and businesses. It's what resonates with you. It's what makes people choose an iPhone over a Samsung and a Mac over a PC.

See how you can bring your unique worldview into your writing, your offers, and your business. You will start to attract people who resonate with your unique worldview.

Constantly flex your idea muscle

Ideas don't resemble creative sparks. Idea generation is also a process, not a magic bullet.

Author and podcaster James Altucher[20] has an interesting concept he calls the idea machine. He tells you to come up with ten ideas every single day. Ten ideas to improve a business. Ten ideas to improve your website. Ten ideas to raise $1,000 in the next ten days. The whole point of this exercise is to push your brain further and continuously strive to innovate.

Believe in selling and keeping promises

Beyond the huge launches, shiny videos, and beautifully designed e-books and websites, you need to sell and keep promises. That should be your main focus, rather than the features of what you're providing. This is one of my favorite quotes from Bernadette Jiwa at The Story of Telling:

"As marketers we often get bogged down in the features and benefits of what it is we have to offer. We get stuck at the telling people what it does part. But here's the thing, deep down most people don't care about what the features enable them to do. Because people don't want to 'do' they want to 'be'. They want to be less busy and more productive, less alone and more connected, less fearful and feel more safe. People don't buy features, they buy promises."

Give yourself permission to say "I don't know"

We are taught that "I don't know" is not an acceptable answer. So we often borrow others' opinions and mask them as our own. Choosing to say "I don't know" forces you to think about what you need to find out more about. It helps you to distill your thoughts.

Believe in opportunity, not competition

Entrepreneurial envy is ruthless. It sneaks up on you when you least expect it.

More subscribers. More followers. More engagement. More money.

It's easy to get sucked into envy. But experts view it as an opportunity. They cheer their peers on and promote and share their work. They believe that the more they give back, the more they get. They build relationships and look for ways to collaborate and form partnerships.

Believe in habits, not motivation

Motivation is unreliable. Even the best of us have uninspiring days. The only way around it? Create habits that become part of your daily activity. Don't bet on motivation to make progress.

Invest in yourself and continuously learn

Develop a system online where you save, clip, or bookmark interesting articles. Tools like Evernote, Skitch, and Pocket are ideal for this. Create time every week to read up on developments in your niche. Identify thought leaders, publications, and leading industry or cross-industry sites in your specialization to read or attend the events of.

Don't be afraid to niche down

Your products, lead magnets, and services are not for everyone, so don't panic when people choose to turn away because they're not the right fit for them. Your audience will self-select as they get to know your brand and your style. Find gaps in the marketplace and stand out there.

Believe in building "100 true email fans"

Don't obsess over follower counts or the latest social media algorithm changes. You don't want to build your following on "rented grounds" such as Facebook or Instagram. Social media is an important part of online business, but you'd rather build 100 true fans on your email list than 10,000 passive followers on a social media network.

Chart your own path rather than blindly following advice

Everyone's business has a different trajectory that is very much dependent on their vision and goals. Maybe you want to work with brands? Or you want to manage content marketing for companies? Or you want to build credibility and go on to establish a consulting business? Study the work of your mentors. But take what you need and chart your own strategy and direction based on that vision.

Solve problems

Even when you write about topics you are passionate about and enjoy, always look to solve problems for your audience. Even a journal style blog detailing your day-to-day activities can provide value if it's written from the angle of helping and answering questions readers have.

Think daily dispatch

How can you capture, share, or implement what you

have read or learned about today?

Use these as a mantra in your own business. Align yourself with them when you have to make a decision about your business. But most importantly, start to implement them on a day-to-day basis because knowledge isn't power until it's applied.

You *can* position yourself as an expert by taking the intentional steps outlined for you in this book. **Remember that people will always pay for expertise and do business with those individuals they know, like, and trust.**

Before you go, I'd like to share one of my favorite quotes with you: "Timing, perseverance, and ten years of trying will eventually make you look like an overnight success." -- *Biz Stone, Co-Founder of Twitter.*

Remember to download your bonuses at **https://nowanexpert.com/bonus.**

Good luck and thank you for sharing your work with the world!

THANK YOU FOR READING

I hope you enjoyed reading this book.

I really appreciate your feedback, and I love hearing what you have to say.

Could you leave me a review on Amazon letting me know what you thought of the book?

Thank you so much! If you want to get in touch, come find me here at my slice of the internet: https://www.meerakothand.com.

Meera

About the Author

Meera Kothand is an email marketing strategist, Amazon best-selling author of the books *The One Hour Content Plan* & *Your First 100*, and founder of CREATE Planners. Her goal is to make powerful marketing strategies simple and relatable so that solopreneurs and small business owners can build a tribe that's addicted to their zone of genius. She has been featured on Smart Blogger, MarketingProfs, YFS Magazine, Addicted2Success, and several other sites.

Other Books on Amazon

RESOURCES

1. Business Dictionary, s.v. "expert (*adj.*)," accessed July 31, 2018, http://www.businessdictionary.com/definition/expert.html.

2. Liam Fitzpatrick, "Micro Influencers vs Macro Influencers: Size Does Matter," *InfluencerBay*, August 2, 2017, https://www.influencerbay.com/blog/micro-influencers-vs-macro-influencers-size-matter/.

3. Colleen Vaughan, "Influencer Marketing Update: Non-Celebrity Influencers 10 Times More Likely to Drive In-Store Purchases," Collective Bias, March 29, 2016, https://collectivebias.com/blog/2016/03/non-celebrity-influencers-drive-store-purchases/.

4. Steve Scott, *How to Find a Profitable Blog Topic Idea (Better Blog Booklets)*, Self-published, Amazon Digital Services, 2014. Kindle, https://www.amazon.com/Find-Profitable-Topic-Better-Booklets-ebook/dp/B00CJBYHJS/.

5. "How Neil Patel Managed to Write 4294 Blog Posts,"

Neil Patel, https://neilpatel.com/blog/blog-consistently/.

6. Perry Marshall, *80/20 Sales and Marketing: The Definitive Guide to Working Less and Making More*, Irvine, CA: Entrepreneur Press, 2013, https://www.amazon.com/80-20-Sales-Marketing-Definitive-ebook/dp/B00CGNRVHE/.

7. AnswerThePublic, https://answerthepublic.com/.

8. Ubersuggest, https://neilpatel.com/ubersuggest/.

9. Nora Aufreiter, Julien Boudet, and Vivian Weng, "Why marketers should keep sending you e-mails," McKinsey, January 2014, https://www.mckinsey.com/business-functions/marketing-and-sales/our-insights/why-marketers-should-keep-sending-you-emails.

10. Matthew Collis, "Why you shouldn't underestimate email marketing: statistics," The American Genius, November 14, 2012, https://theamericangenius.com/business-

marketing/why-you-shouldnt-underestimate-the-value-of-email-marketing/.

11. BuzzSumo, http://buzzsumo.com/.

12. The Story of Telling, https://thestoryoftelling.com/.

13. Steven Pressfield, *The War of Art: Break Through the Blocks and Win Your Inner Creative Battles*, New York: Black Irish Entertainment, 2012, https://www.amazon.com/War-Art-Through-Creative-Battles/dp/1936891026.

14. "Content Curation: Why Is The Content Curator The Key Emerging Online Editorial Role Of The Future?," MasterNewMedia, January 20, 2010, https://www.masternewmedia.org/content-curation-why-is-the-content-curator-the-key-emerging-online-editorial-role-of-the-future/#ixzz5LxOE9D2g.

15. *Oxford Dictionary*, s.v. "influence (*n.*)," accessed July 31, 2018, https://en.oxforddictionaries.com/definition/influence.

16. Robert Cialdini, *Influence: The Psychology of Persuasion*, rev. ed., New York: Harper Business, 2006, https://www.amazon.com/Influence-Psychology-Persuasion-Robert-Cialdini/dp/006124189X/.

17. Jacob Neilson, "How Long Do Users Stay on Web Pages?", *Neilson Norman Group*, September 12, 2011, https://www.nngroup.com/articles/how-long-do-users-stay-on-web-pages/.

18. "Five-Second Testing," *Usability Hub*, https://usabilityhub.com/guides/five-second-testing.

19. Donald Miller, *Building a StoryBrand: Clarify Your Message So Customers Will Listen*, Nashville: HarperCollins Leadership, 2017, https://www.amazon.com/Building-StoryBrand-Clarify-Message-Customers/dp/0718033329 .

20. "The Ultimate Guide for Becoming an Idea Machine," *James Altucher*, https://jamesaltucher.com/2014/05/the-ultimate-guide-for-becoming-an-idea-machine/.

Made in the USA
Lexington, KY
18 June 2019